# KING ST.

Set Two
BOOK 8

# Falling Out

*Falling Out*
King Street: Readers Set Two - Book 8
Copyright © Iris Nunn 2014

Text: Iris Nunn
Editor: June Lewis
Illustrations: Pip Jones and Marta Kwasniewska

Published in 2014 by Gatehouse Media Limited

ISBN: 978-1-84231-123-3

*British Library Cataloguing-in-Publication Data:*
A catalogue record for this book is available from the British Library

Students live at number five,
three students,
Ros, Sally and Kate.

Steve used to live there,
but he left.

He got a job.
He cooks in a pub in town.
Now he lives over the pub,
in a flat.

Kate lives at number five now.
At first things were fine.
The three girls got on very well.

Now it's a disaster!

The thing is this:

Kate will not clear up after herself.
She leaves dishes on the table.
She leaves pans on the cooker.
She leaves pots in the sink.
The floor is dirty.
The table is dirty.
The kitchen's a mess!

Now, Ros and Sally get on well.
At first they got on well with Kate,
but now they will not speak to Kate.

They are waiting for Kate
to clear up her mess!

Then Ros has a good idea.

Kate likes Steve,
Steve who used to live here.
She fancies him.

"Let's ask him round!" said Ros.
They told Kate.

Well, that did the trick.

Kate cleaned the dishes.
She cleaned the pans.
She cleaned the pots.
She cleaned the floor.
She cleaned the table.

The kitchen looked clean
and bright!

Ros smiled at Sally.
"That was a good idea!"

And now Steve has moved back into number five.

# KING ST.

## Set Two
## BOOK 2

## Neeta Volunteers

*Neeta Volunteers*
King Street: Readers Set Two - Book 2
Copyright © Iris Nunn 2014

Text: Iris Nunn
Editor: June Lewis
Illustrations: Pip Jones and Marta Kwasniewska

Published in 2014 by Gatehouse Media Limited

ISBN: 978-1-84231-117-2

*British Library Cataloguing-in-Publication Data:*
A catalogue record for this book is available from the British Library

Neeta lives at number nine.

Her children are grown up.

She cleans the house,
she keeps the garden tidy,
but she is a bit bored.

She would like a job.

One day her husband,
Kuldip, says to her,

"Why don't you become
a volunteer?
There are lots of things
you could do."

"You could help at the school.
You could help at the hospital.
You could help at the college.
You could help at the nursing home."

Neeta thinks about it.

She goes to find out
about volunteer work.

So now Neeta helps
at Kingsmead Hospital.
She helps in the café.

She enjoys her job.

"I feel useful now."

# KING ST.

## Set Two
## BOOK 6

---

# Becky and Will

---

*Becky and Will*
King Street: Readers Set Two - Book 6
Copyright © Iris Nunn 2014

Text: Iris Nunn
Editor: June Lewis
Illustrations: Pip Jones and Marta Kwasniewska

Published in 2014 by Gatehouse Media Limited

ISBN: 978-1-84231-121-9

*British Library Cataloguing-in-Publication Data:*
A catalogue record for this book is available from the British Library

Last week the new people moved
into number eight.

They came in a small van.

They had a bed.

They had a cooker.

They had a sofa.

They had some chairs.

They had some rugs.

They had a cat.

"No kids," said June
of number nineteen.

"A cat," said Sam.
"Look out, Jim.
No chasing it!"

"A bit posh," said Dave.

"They look nice," said Gwen
of number eleven.

"Would you like a cup of tea?"
said Jill.

So Becky and Will popped next door
to Jill's house.

"I'm a teacher," said Becky.
"My first job."

"And I'm still a student," said Will.
"We met at college."

"Nice to meet you," said Jill.
"I hope you'll be happy
in King Street."

Becky popped into the corner shop for some milk.

"I hope you'll be happy here," said Mrs T.

That evening they called into the pub
for a drink.

"Nice to meet you," said Brenda.
"I hope you'll be happy here.
Have this round on the house."

# KING ST.

## Set Two
## BOOK 7

# Locked Out

*Locked Out*
King Street: Readers Set Two - Book 7
Copyright © Iris Nunn 2014

Text: Iris Nunn
Editor: June Lewis
Illustrations: Pip Jones and Marta Kwasniewska

Published in 2014 by Gatehouse Media Limited

ISBN: 978-1-84231-122-6

*British Library Cataloguing-in-Publication Data:*
A catalogue record for this book is available from the British Library

Sam is getting on.
He forgets things.

Last week he forgot his key.
He felt in his pockets,
all his pockets.

He went next door
to number eight.

He rang the bell.
He waited.
He waited and waited.

Then he heard a bell,
a bell from the street.

Along came Will on his bike.

"Hello, Sam," said Will,
"What can I do for you?"

Sam told him about the key.
He told him he was locked out.

"We'll have a cup of tea
then we'll see if we can get in,"
said Will.

So Sam and Jim went
into number eight
and Will made a cup of tea.

After tea Will got a screwdriver.
They went out of the back door
and round into Sam's back yard.

"I don't think I'll need this,"
said Will.

Upstairs there was an open window,
the bathroom window.

"Have you got a ladder?"
said Will.

Up he went and in he got.

In no time he was opening
the back door for Sam.

"You might think I was used to this,"
said Will with a smile.

"It's good to have neighbours," said Sam. "Thanks, Will."